Snap books™
Cheerleading

Cheer Tryouts

Making the Cut

by Jen Jones

Capstone press

Mankato, Minnesota

Snap Books are published by Capstone Press,
151 Good Counsel Drive, P.O. Box 669, Mankato, Minnesota 56002
www.capstonepress.com

Library of Congress Cataloging-in-Publication Data
Jones, Jen, 1976-
  Cheer tryouts: making the cut / by Jen Jones.
    p. cm. — (Snap books cheerleading)
  Includes bibliographical references and index.
  ISBN 0-7368-4361-2 (hardcover)
  1. Cheerleading — Juvenile literature. I. Title. II. Series.
  LB3635.J66 2006
  791.6'4 — dc22   2005007266

Summary: A guide for children and pre-teens on preparing for
cheerleading tryouts.

Editor: Deb Berry/Bill SMITH STUDIO
Illustrators: Lisa Parett; Roxanne Daner, Marina Terletsky and Brock Waldron/Bill SMITH STUDIO
Designers: Marina Terletsky, and Brock Waldron/Bill SMITH STUDIO
Photo Researcher: Iris Wong/Bill SMITH STUDIO

Photo Credits: Cover: Bob Daemmrich/The Image Works; 8, Syracuse Newspapers/Suzanne Dunn/The Image Works;
12, (bl) Artville, (r) PhotoDisc; 13, (bg) Darren Modricker/Corbis, (tr & br) PhotoDisc;
19, Brand X Pictures/Getty Images; 20, BananaStock/Superstock; 32, Britton Lenahan.
Back Cover, Getty Images. All other photos by Tim Jackson photography.

1 2 3 4 5 6 10 09 08 07 06 05

Table of Contents

So, You Want to Be A Cheerleader

Have you always been drawn in by the excitement of cheerleading? You're not alone. There are more than 3 million cheerleaders in the United States!

Gone are the days when cheerleaders simply shook their pom-poms to root for sports teams. Tumbling, stunting, and dancing are all part of modern cheerleading, which has gained respect as a sport and draws big crowds.

4

As a cheerleader, you'll perform for crowds and raise school spirit. You'll also be counted on to act as a role model for the kids at school and the community. It may seem like a lot to deal with, but you'll have your teammates supporting you all the way. Plus, don't forget all the extras. You'll make new friends, get great exercise, and gain a whole new set of skills!

But before you can cheer, you need to make the team. This book lets you in on all the big secrets for a successful tryout.

So what are you waiting for? Let's get started!

Getting Off on the Right Foot

Have you heard the saying, "The early bird gets the worm?" That might sound disgusting, but it has a grain of truth. The earlier you start preparing for spring tryouts, the better your chances of wearing a uniform in the fall.

One sure ticket to success is to watch the **squad** in action during the school year. Studying the **routines** can give you a good idea of the moves you will have to perform at tryout time.

Another trick is to start training on your own. Sign up for local dance and gymnastics classes. Stay active and stretch out regularly to keep your body in the best shape possible.

Preparing for tryouts is almost like getting ready to run in a marathon. Smart preparation will make you feel more sure about meeting the challenge. Train your heart out. You'll have a blast, and your body will thank you!

"Start training on your own."

Got Skills?

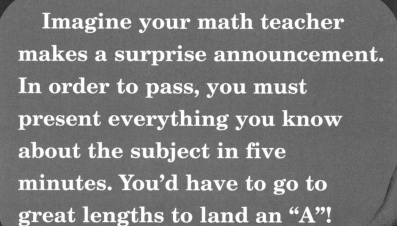

Imagine your math teacher makes a surprise announcement. In order to pass, you must present everything you know about the subject in five minutes. You'd have to go to great lengths to land an "A"!

You've just imagined what cheer tryouts are like. This is your chance to shine for the judges. To prove that you've got what it takes to represent the school as a cheerleader, you'll be asked to perform the following skills.

Motions These arm movements are used in cheers and dance routines.

Jumps Common jumps include toe touches, herkies, hurdlers, pikes, and tucks.

Tumbling Cheerleading tryouts usually include splits, cartwheels, and **round-offs**. As "extra credit," you can perform **walkovers, handsprings,** or **flips**.

Cheers and Chants These are ways to lead the crowd using your voice and cheer moves.

Dance Routines Learned in counts of eight, these routines use motions, jumps, and dance moves for visual effect.

Tricks to Get You in Tip-Top Tryout Shape

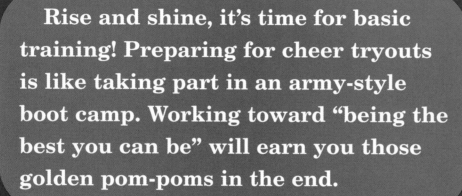

Rise and shine, it's time for basic training! Preparing for cheer tryouts is like taking part in an army-style boot camp. Working toward "being the best you can be" will earn you those golden pom-poms in the end.

On that note, gathering the troops is also helpful (and fun!). Persuade friends to train with you a few times a week. As "war buddies," you can support each other in the battle to make the team. Future cheerleaders, stick together!

Atten-TION! Basic Training
Step 1. Stretch often to increase your flexibility

Flexibility is the key to better jumps, gymnastics, and splits. The best way to become more flexible is to stretch out properly and often. Stretching helps get rid of stiff muscles and lowers your chances of getting hurt. The best part is that you can stretch anytime, even while you're watching television or talking on the phone.

Step 2, Practice "plyometrics" for the highest jumps

Say what? **Plyometrics** are exercises that will make your jumps higher and stronger, giving you more bounce. Even simple exercises like jumping rope or jumping jacks count.

Step 3. Eat right for energy

Just as expensive cars use costly fuel, a fit body needs healthy foods for energy. Think of breakfast as your morning fuel. For that first burst of energy to start your day, try a bagel topped with peanut butter. Throughout the rest of the day, snacks like string cheese and fruit can also give you a lift.

Step 4. Put motion drills in motion.

Run through a full set of motions once a day, keeping your movements sharp. If practicing with friends, form a single-file line and call out each motion. When this drill is done correctly, everyone's arms should be perfectly in line.

The Scoop on Tryout Clinics

As tryout time nears, all cheer wannabes must attend a one-week series of classes known as "clinics." There you'll learn all the material that you'll need to know for tryouts. In other words, clinics are serious stuff!

While learning tryout routines, pay attention to the instructors and copy their movements. Don't be afraid to ask questions. Learning cheers the right way the first time is a must. When you're all by yourself on the tryout floor, you'll be thankful you remember everything correctly.

At clinics, the instructors are often graduating cheerleaders on the lookout for talented new members. If you ask them what to expect, odds are they'll be happy to share their wisdom! You should also take time to get to know the team coach. He or she will be watching all week to see how well people get along and listen to direction. Playing hooky is *not* encouraged. Use this chance to show your talent *and* your spirit!

"Clinics are serious stuff!"

Practice Makes Perfect

Think of tryout week as a countdown to the big day. Every minute counts. At clinics, you'll be learning lots of new information. Whether in your backyard, on the playground, or in your head, take advantage of spare time to review what you've learned.

Practice doesn't have to be a chore. Find strength in numbers and invite friends to make practice more like a party. Since you've all learned the same material, now is the time to help each other perfect your moves. Use the mirror to see how your cheers look when performed next to others. For added fun, practice jumps on a trampoline. Just make sure you have an adult to spot you.

At the end of the week, some coaches may offer a "mock tryout." (Luckily, scores don't count.) You'll be asked to perform tryout skills and will be given a score sheet with feedback. Use it as a gold mine of information to find out what you should improve on before tryouts.

"Make practice more like a party!"

Take a Chill Pill

Pair lots of practicing with a strong dream of "making it," and it's enough to worry even the calmest of cheer hopefuls! If you're feeling unusually anxious, check out these great ways to relax before the big tryout.

* When you start to worry too much, shut your eyes and breathe deeply three times.

* Don't overdo it on practice. If you run yourself ragged before tryouts, you won't be at your personal best when the day finally comes. Know your body's limits and stick to them!

* Let loose with a slumber party. Invite friends over for practice, followed by munchies, manicures, and movies. Just don't stay up *too* late!

It's also important to keep an open mind. No matter what happens at tryouts, take comfort in knowing that you are fully prepared and tried your best. All the practice and stretching has probably improved your health and skills. Now that's something to cheer about!

'Twas the Night Before Tryouts

'Twas the night before tryouts
And in the heart of the town
A future cheerleader lay awake
hoping she was squad-bound.

The pom-poms were hung by the nightstand with care
In hopes that a uniform would soon join them there.
She'd practiced non-stop for weeks on end
And was finally resting so her body could mend.

Too wired to sleep
Too tired to practice
Counting sheep did nothing
As she tossed and turned on the mattress.

Finally she managed to fall asleep
Her night dreams were filled with tryout rules to keep.

Sharp motions! Be confident! Stay focused! Stay riled!
Be a dancer! Be a gymnast! And don't forget to SMILE!

The judges watched with patience and glee
As she showed off her stuff for everyone to see.
They scribbled on their pads
Notes feverish and fast
Until they raised up their scorecards
Reading perfect 10s — she passed!

Just as she reached for the golden cheer crown
Her alarm clock went off
Waking her with the loud sound.
She smiled and stretched
Thinking of the challenge ahead.
Her mom stood above her with the rest of her fam.

"Are you ready for the big day, honey?"
"Yes, I am!"

21

Trying Out with Pizzazz and All That Jazz

> You only have a few minutes to convince the judges that you belong on the team. Use your time wisely.

Tryout Dos and Don'ts

Don't wear baggy or untucked clothing. The judges can't see your motions clearly if you're sporting sloppy sweats!

Do look presentable with a clean T-shirt and gym shorts. Long hair should be in a ponytail and makeup kept minimal and classy.

Don't freak out if you mess up. The judges will be watching to see how you deal with mistakes. If you mess up, simply smile and keep on going. It's all about staying calm and collected!

Do enter the room with lots of energy. Hands on hips, smiles on lips!

Don't try to figure out what the judges are thinking. Their job is to stay fair, meaning they can't smile at or encourage anyone. Stay in the zone!

Do show your belief in yourself. If you believe that you can do it, the judges will, too!

23

Sneak Peek Inside the Judge's Head

We sent out our trusted cheer spies to find out exactly what judges look for during tryouts. See their findings below.

Spirit and Showmanship

* Big, natural smiles
* Pep and a good attitude
* A love of performing
* Looking judges in the eyes
* How your face changes during routines
* How you handle your mistakes

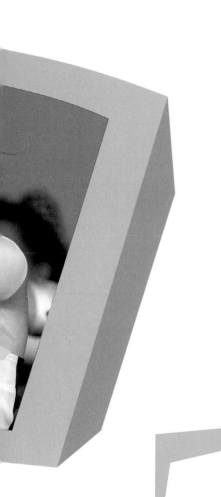

Appearance
* Well-kept, polished look
* The right clothing choices

Voice
* Yelling loudly and clearly
* Breath control
* No rushing, high-pitched tones, or shrieking

Motions
* Clean, crisp arm movements
* Knowledge of the motions

Dance
* Rhythm
* Ability to remember combinations
* No mouthing the counts

Jumps and Splits
* Height of jumps
* Knowledge and ability to perform different jumps
* How far down are your splits? Are your toes pointed?

Gymnastics
* Strong basic gymnastic skills
* Ability to learn new skills
* If advanced, are you performing skills safely and correctly?

The Moment of Cheer Truth, Making the Squad

The good news. You've done everything you can do. The bad news. Now you have to wait for the decision!

All coaches have a different system for announcing who will be on the new team. Some coaches read out names immediately after tryouts, while other coaches call everyone personally with the good or bad news. No matter how decisions are delivered, it's always nerve-wracking as scores are added. After all, you've spent a lot of time preparing for this moment! It's only natural to hope for the best.

Keep in mind that not everyone will make the team. You could land a spot on the squad, but your friends may not. Or the opposite might happen. The sting may present a small challenge to your friendship, but it's only fair to wish each other well. You don't want to put down anyone's hard work. At the core of cheerleading is good sportsmanship, and that carries over to real life!

If you made the team, congratulations! You're about to set off on an amazing adventure. Cheerleading is an exciting and demanding sport that builds friendships and new skills. If you haven't made the team, turn the page.

If At First You Don't Succeed, Try, Try Again

A Note from Jen

I'll never forget cheerleading tryouts at the end of my second year in high school. I was a junior varsity cheerleader and hoping to bump up to the varsity squad. The problem? Six other junior varsity cheerleaders were trying out for three available spots. (And that didn't even count the new people trying out!)

I've never worked so hard to prepare for something. For the entire spring, I jumped, stretched, danced, and cheered nonstop. I wanted it so bad, I could taste it. On the morning of

tryouts, my mom left me a batch of Rice Krispies Treats with an encouraging note. It gave me the extra courage I needed to go in there and knock 'em dead.

Unfortunately, when the results were read, I heard my name called out, but for *junior* varsity. I was heartbroken. Why wasn't I picked for varsity? But it wasn't the end of the world. Though I wasn't a varsity cheerleader, my junior year of cheering was still amazing! I was elected co-captain and was named an all-star at cheerleading camp. Senior year, I finally landed that hard-to-get varsity spot.

Sometimes we want something so much that we lose sight of what's important. If you want to be a cheerleader badly enough, odds are you will make the squad someday. If it doesn't happen the first time, you might need an extra year of practice. But it's okay. No one thinks any less of you. It takes a lot of courage to try out. Some adults can't even speak in front of a crowd, let alone yell, jump, and dance! Pat yourself on the back for giving your all and promise yourself you'll try again. You owe yourself at least that much.

Cheers,

Jen Jones

GLOSSARY

clinic (KLIN-ik) a group lesson where cheerleading skills for tryouts are taught

competition (kom-puh-TISH-uhn) a contest in which two or more people are trying to win the same thing

essentials (uh-SEN-shuls) necessary items that someone can't do without

flexibility (FLEK-suh-buhl-i-tee) being able to bend and stretch without getting hurt

flip (FLIP) gymnastic trick in which the body does a full 360-degree turn in the air

handspring (HAND-spring) like a flip, but hands touch ground at midway point

plyometrics (PLYE-o-met-riks) exercises which can lead to higher and stronger jumps

round-off (ROUND-awf) a more powerful version of a cartwheel

routine (roo-TEEN) a set of cheers and chants performed in order, or a dance number to chosen music

squad (SKWAHD) a team of cheerleaders

varsity (VAR-suh-tee) the senior sports team that represents the school

FAST FACTS

First Impressions Count

Statistics show that appearance and body language are the first things we notice about other people, so keep that in mind when in front of the tryout judges!

Back in the Saddle

Though comfortable sneakers are on everyone's feet these days, saddle shoes were the shoe of choice until the 1970s.

READ MORE

Golden, Suzi J. and Roger Schreiber. *101 Best Cheers: How to Be the Best Cheerleader Ever*. New York: Troll Communications, 2001.

McElroy, James T. *We've Got Spirit: The Life and Times of America's Greatest Cheerleading Team*. New York: Berkley Publishing Group, 2000.

Neil, Randy and Elaine Hart. *The Official Cheerleader's Handbook*. New York: Fireside, 1986.

Peters, Craig. *Competitive Cheerleading*. Broomall, Pennsylvania: Mason Crest, 2003.

Wilson, Leslie. *The Ultimate Guide to Cheerleading*. New York: Three Rivers Press, 2003.

INTERNET SITES

FactHound offers a safe, fun way to find Internet sites related to this book. All of the sites on FactHound have been researched by our staff.

Here's how

1. Visit *www.facthound.com*

2. Type in this special code **0736843612** for age-appropriate sites. Or enter a search word related to this book for a more general search.

3. Click on the **Fetch It** button. FactHound will fetch the best sites for you!

ABOUT THE AUTHOR

While growing up in Ohio, Jen Jones spent seven years as a cheerleader for her grade-school and high-school squads. Following high school, she coached several cheer squads to team victory. For two years, she also cheered and created dance numbers for the Chicago Lawmen semi-professional football dance team.

Jen gets her love of cheerleading honestly, because her mother, sister, and cousins are also heavily involved in the sport! As well as teaching occasional dance and cheerleading workshops, Jen now works in sunny Los Angeles as a freelance writer for publications like *American Cheerleader* and *Dance Spirit*.

Index